That Was Then

That Was Then

Gerard Stembridge

Methuen Drama

Published by Methuen 2002

1 3 5 7 9 10 8 6 4 2

First published in 2002 by
Methuen Publishing Limited,
215 Vauxhall Bridge Road,
London SW1V 1EJ

Methuen Publishing Limited Reg. No. 3543167

A CIP catalogue record is available from the British Library

ISBN 0 413 77262 4

Typeset by SX Composing DTP, Rayleigh, Essex
Printed and bound in Great Britain by
Cox & Wyman Ltd, Reading, Berkshire

The National Theatre
The Abbey and Peacock Theatres

That was Then

By Gerard Stembridge

The National Theatre gratefully acknowledges the financial
support from the Arts Council/An Chomhairle Ealaíon

That was Then

By Gerard Stembridge

That was Then by Gerard Stembridge was first performed at the Abbey Theatre on Thursday 16 May 2002. Press night was 21 May 2002.

The play is set somewhat in the past and slightly in the future

There will be one interval of 15 minutes

Cast

Noel	Stephen Brennan
May	Marion O'Dwyer
Julian	Nick Dunning
June	Julia Lane
April	Jade Yourell
Director	Gerard Stembridge
Designer	Es Devlin
Lighting Designer	Paul Keogan
Assistant Director	David Horan
Sound	Eddie Breslin
Stage Director	John Stapleton
Assistant Stage Manager	Catriona Behan
Voice Coach	Andrea Ainsworth
Set	Abbey Theatre Workshop
Costumes	Abbey Theatre Wardrobe Department

Please note that the text of the play which appears in this volume may be changed during the rehearsal process and appear in a slightly altered form in performance.

Gerard Stembridge *Author and Director*

Gerard Stembridge is a writer and director. He has written theatre plays, **Lovechild, The Gay Detective** and **Denis and Rose,** television dramas, **The Truth about Claire** and **Black Day at Black Rock** and radio plays, **Daisy the Cow who Talked** and **Daylight Robbery.** His films are **Guiltrip** and **About Adam** and his screen plays are **Ordinary Decent Criminal** and **Nora** (co-written with Pat Murphy).

Es Devlin *Designer*

Es trained at Bristol University, Central Saint Martins and Motley Theatre Design Course. Theatre designs include **Hinterland,** Abbey Theatre, Royal National Theatre, Out of Joint, **Anthony and Cleopatra,** RSC, **Arabian Night,** Soho Theatre, **A Day in the Death of Joe Egg,** New Ambassadors, **The Prisoner's Dilemma,** RSC, **Meat,** Theatre Royal, Plymouth (Nominated for TMA 2001 Best Design Award), **Howie the Rookie,** Bush Theatre (Winner of TMA 1999 Best Design Award), **Henry IV,** RSC, **Betrayal,** RNT, **Rita, Sue and Bob Too/A State Affair,** Out of Joint/Soho Theatre, **Hamlet,** Young Vic, Tokyo Globe, **Credible Witness, Yard Gal,** Royal Court, **Snake in the Grass,** Old Vic, **Piano,** TPT, Tokyo, **Love and Understanding, Love You Too, One Life and Counting, Drink, Dance, Laugh, Lie,** Bush Theatre, **Perapalas,** Gate Theatre, **The Death of Cool,** Hampstead Theatre, **Closer to Heaven,** Arts Theatre, **Edward II,** Bolton Octagon, (Winner of the 1995 Linbury Prize for Stage Design). Opera designs include **Hansel and Gretel,** Scottish Opera Go Round, **Fidelio,** English Touring Opera, **Powder Her Face,** Ystad Festival, Sweden, **Don Giovanni,** British Youth Opera. Designs for dance include **A Streetcar Named Desire,** Northern Ballet Theatre, **God's Plenty** and **Four Scenes** both for Rambert Dance Company. Designs for film include **Brilliant!, Ten by Ten** for BBC2, **A Tale of Two Heads, Beggars Belief, Snow on Saturday** (winner of the Kino Best British Short Film 2001).

Paul Keogan *Lighting Designer*

Born in Dublin Paul studied Drama at The Samuel Beckett Centre, Trinity College Dublin and at Glasgow University. After graduating Paul worked as Production Manager for Project Arts Centre. He has designed a number of productions for the Abbey and Peacock Theatres including **Melonfarmer, The Electrocution of Children, Amazing Grace, Living Quarters, Making History, The Map Maker's Sorrow, Cúirt an Mheán Oíche, Treehouses, Mrs Warren's Profession, Bailegangaire, The Sanctuary Lamp, The Morning After Optimism, The Tempest, Tartuffe** and **Eden**. Other designs include **The Silver Tassie**, Almeida Theatre, London, **The Gay Dectective**, Project, **Quay West** and **Blasted**, Bedrock Productions, **Ballads**, **Seasons** and **The Rite of Spring**, CoisCéim Dance Theatre, **Lady Macbeth** of Mtsensk and **The Silver Tassie**, Opera Ireland, **The Lighthouse**, Opera Theatre Company, **The Makropulos Case**, Opera Zuid, Netherlands, **SAMO**, Block & Steel, Netherlands, **Too Late for Logic**, Edinburgh International Festival, **Olga**, Traverse Theatre, Edinburgh, **Denis and Rose**, Civic Theatre Tallaght, **The Wishing Well**, a large scale outdoor projection piece for Kilkenny Arts Festival 1999 and most recently, **The Gates of Gold** for the Gate Theatre.

Stephen Brennan *Noel*

Stephen's most recent appearances at the Abbey Theatre were as Harry in **The Sanctuary Lamp**, Kearns in **A Life** and Henry in **The Wake**. He spent several years in musicals before joining the Abbey Theatre in 1976, where he played more than sixty leading and supporting roles, including the title role in **Hamlet**. He joined the Royal National Theatre, London in 1983 and apart from Frank'n'Furter in **The Rocky Horror Show** and Petruchio in **The Taming of the Shrew**, has worked almost exclusively at the Gate since 1988, where roles include Lord Goring in **An Ideal Husband**, Elyot in **Private Lives**, Lucky in **Waiting for Godot**, the title role in Moliere's **Tartuffe**, Oberon/Theseus in **A Midsummer Night's Dream**, Serge in **Art**, Cyrano in **Cyrano de Bergerac** and the title role of **Oedipus** at the Gaiety. Film work includes **Eat the Peach** and **The General**. His television work includes **El Cid**, the second series of **Ballykissangel**, **Father Ted**, **DDU**, **Mystic Knights**, **A Piece of Monologue** and **Waiting for Godot** for the Beckett Film Project. He most recently appeared at the Gate Theatre in **Two Plays** by Brian Friel

Nick Dunning *Julian*

Nick's previous appearances at the Abbey and Peacock Theatres include **Mrs Warren's Profession**, **The Marriage of Figaro** and **The Last Ones**. Recently he appeared in **The Homecoming** by Pinter at the Gate Theatre also in New York at the Lincoln Center, Pinter Festival and a long run in London's West End.   Other theatre work includes **The Strongest Man in the World**, Lincoln Center, New York, **Some Explicit Polaroids**, Out of Joint, **No Man's Land**, Gate Theatre, **A Handful of Dust**, **Comedy without a Title**, **Marriage**, **Successful Stratagems**, **False Admissions**, Shared Experience, **Othello**, Lyric Hammersmith, **The**

Taming of the Shrew, The Happy End, Royal Shakespeare Company, **The Wandering Jew, Countrymania, Richard II,** Royal National Theatre, **Glasshouses, The Recruiting Officer, Our Country's Good, Doing the Business, Beside Herself,** Royal Court Theatre, **Phoenix,** Bush Theatre, **According to Hoyle,** Hampstead Theatre. Television credits include **Remembrance, Strangers, The Young Ones, Way Upstream, The Firm, The Bill, Saracen, El Cid, The Rory Bremner Show, The Roughest Way, The Rita Rudner Show, Events at Drimagleen, Alive and Kicking, Resnick, Minder II, Boon, Casualty, Between the Lines, Sister My Sister, Medics, A Few Short Journeys of the Heart, Drop the Dead Donkey, Wycliffe, Sharman, Into the Blue, Making the Cut, The Ambassador, Midsomer Murders, Vanity Fair, Surgical Two, Dangerfield** and **Ultimate Force.** Films include **Lamb, London Kills Me, The Fifth Province, Jackie Chan's Highbinders** and he has just completed **East of Harlem** with Jim Sheridan.

Julia Lane *June*

Since graduating from Oxford University and The Drama Studio Julia has worked extensively in theatre and television. She last appeared at the Abbey and Peacock Theatres in **Blackwater Angel** by Jim Nolan. Other theatre work includes **The Homecoming,** Leicester Haymarket, **The Positive Hour,** Out of Joint, **Gaucho, The Fancy Man,** Hampstead Theatre, **The Rover,** RSC, **Jane Eyre,** Birmingham Rep, **The Changeling, Macbeth,** Contact Theatre, **Abolition,** Bristol Old Vic. Television credits include **Ballykissangel, Prime Suspect V, Thieftakers, Heartbeat, Capital City, Achilles Heel, Inspector Morse, Brighton Belles, A Pinch of Snuff, The Sharp End, The Bill, Casualty** and **Boon.** Films include **Woman at War, Memories of Midnight, The Secret Rapture** and **Black Eyes.**

Marion O'Dwyer *May*

Marion's previous appearances at the Abbey and Peacock Theatres include **En Suite, The Memory of Water, Kevin's Bed, The Only True History of Lizzie Finn, Portia Coughlan** at the Peacock and the Royal Court, London, **Moving, You Can't Take it with You, The Silver Tassie** and **Dancing at Lughnasa** which also toured Ireland and Australia and **Wonderful Tennessee** in which she also played on Broadway. Appearances at the Gate Theatre include Stella in **Stella by Starlight, A Tale of Two Cities, Pride and Prejudice, The Threepenny Opera, Fathers and Sons, Blithe Spirit, Twelfth Night** and **An Ideal Husband.** For Druid Theatre Company she played in **The Donahue Sisters, Lovers' Meeting,**

Poor Beast in the Rain and **The Loves of Cass Maguire**. Other theatre work includes Molly in **Molly Sweeney** for the Bristol Old Vic, Mena in **Sive** at the Watford Palace Theatre and Tricycle Theatre, London, Liz in **From Both Hips** for Fishamble Theatre Company at project @ the mint and the Tron Theatre, Glasgow. Marion co-starred in Anjelica Houston's film **Agnes Browne**. Other film and television work includes Oonagh in **Ballykissangel**, appearances in **The Ambassador, Rebel Heart, The Life of Reilly, Finbarr's Class** and **Thou shalt not Kill**. Marion's radio work includes the recent BBC Radio 4 series **Faithful Departed** and she was a member of the RTE Players for four years. She also directed **Long Lonely Time** at Andrews Lane Theatre.

Jade Yourell *April*

Jade trained at the Ann Kavanagh Young People's Theatre and D.I.T. Rathmines. This is her first appearance at the Abbey and Peacock Theatres. Other theatre work includes Thomasina in Tom Stoppard's **Arcadia,** directed by Ben Barnes. Mabel Chiltern in **An Ideal Husband,** directed by Alan Stanford at the Gate Theatre and **The Importance of Being Earnest,** Town Hall Theatre. Jade can currently be seen as Jasmine Conoly in **Fair City** (RTE).

Amharclann Na Mainistreach
The National Theatre

SPONSORS

Aer Lingus
Anglo Irish Bank
Ferndale Films
Dr. A. J. F. O'Reilly
RTE
Smurfit Ireland Ltd
The Gulbenkian Foundation
The Irish Times

BENEFACTORS

Aer Rianta
AIB Group
An Post
Bank of Ireland
Behaviour and Attitudes
Electricity Supply Board
Independent News and Media, PLC
IIB Bank
Irish Life & Permanent plc
Pfizer International Bank Europe
Scottish Provident Ireland
SDS
SIPTU
Unilever Ireland Plc

PATRONS

J. G. Corry
Guinness Ireland Group
Irish Actors Equity
Gerard Kelly & Co
McCullough-Mulvin Architects
Mercer Ltd
Smurfit Corrugated Cases
Sumitomo Mitsui Finance (Dublin)
Total Print and Design
Francis Wintle

**SPONSORS OF THE NATIONAL
THEATRE ARCHIVE**

Jane & James O'Donoghue
Sarah & Michael O'Reilly
Rachel & Victor Treacy

FRIENDS OF THE ABBEY

Margaret Ball
Patricia Barnett
Mr. Ron Bolger
Mr. Hugh Boyle
Mrs. Patricia Browne
Mr. Bernard Brogan

Ms. Ann Byrne
Mr. Joseph Byrne
Ms. Zita Byrne
Ann & Eamonn Cantwell
Lilian & Robert Chambers
Ms. Orla Cleary
Claire Cronin
Mrs. Dolores Deacon
Paul & Janet Dempsey
Patricia Devlin
Karen Doull
Pauline Fitzpatrick
Paul & Florence Flynn
Ms. Christina Goldrick
Leslie Greer
Mrs. Rosaleen Hardiman
Sean & Mary Holahan
Brian Hewson
Elizabeth Horkan
Mrs. Madeleine Humphreys
Ms. Eileen Jackson
Ms. Kate Kavanagh
Mr. Francis Keenan
Mr. Peter Keenan
Vivienne & Kieran Kelly
Joan & Michael Keogh
Donal & Mâire Lowry
Mr. Fechin Maher
Una M. Moran
McCann FitzGerald Solicitors
Padraig McCartan
Ms. Ellie McCullough
Mr. Joseph McCullough
Marcella & Aidan McDonnell
Berna McMenamin
Dr. Chris Morash
Mr. Frank Murray
Ann Nolan
Giuliano Nistri
Donal O'Buachalla
Paul O'Doherty
Mrs. Mary O'Driscoll
Ann O'Kennedy
Eugene O'Sullivan
Mr Dermot & Ita O'Sullivan
Mr. Vincent O'Doherty
Mr. Andrew Parkes
Dr. Colette Pegum
Mr. Michael P. Quinn
Yvonne Redmond
Lillian Rohan
Mr. Noel Ryan
Breda & Brendan Shortall
Fr. Frank Stafford
Don & Maura Thornhill
Nuala Ward

Amharclann Na Mainistreach
The National Theatre

For my father,
Tony Stembridge

*The play is set in two time periods simultaneously: 'Not so long ago'
and 'Some time in the future'. There is five or six years between them.
The Action in both time periods is continuous on stage. There are no
freezes, no lights down on one side while action continues on the other.
Where there is an extended sequence in one time period I try to indicate
what action is happening in the other. To facilitate easier reading the
'Not so long ago' sections are boxed.*

'Not so long ago' in Dublin, **Noel** *and* **May Gregory**, *an Irish
married couple, are hosting a meal with two strangers, an English
couple* **Julian** *and* **June Summers.** *It is primarily a business
thing,* **Julian** *having been recommended to* **Noel** *as someone who can
help him get round a problem.*

Some time in the future in London, **Julian** *and* **June** *are preparing to
return the compliment. They have not seen* **Noel** *or* **May** *since that
dinner party in Dublin. Now circumstances have changed.* **Noel**
appears to have become extraordinarily successful while **Julian** *and*
June *urgently need help.*

*The set has two kitchens, Dublin and London right and left, with a
dining room centre. The single dining room serves for both Dublin and
London. As should one front entrance.*

May *is in her kitchen, preparing food, humming happily.* **Julian** *sits
slumped in his dark kitchen, a newspaper spread out on the table in
front of him.* **Noel** *arrives bearing a crate of wine. He enters the
dining room.*

May   Noel, Noel!

June *arrives carrying a briefcase and also enters the dining room.
Stands next to* **Noel**.

Noel   Yes.

June   I'm home.

May   Is that you, Noel?

Noel   Have a guess, May?

June *sees a plastic shopping bag on the floor. She picks it up.*

Noel *sets the wine crate on the table.*

June   Darling?

May   Was Mammy in good form?

Noel   If you mean does she mind looking after the kids tonight, she's thrilled.

May   Ah great.

June (*checking watch*)   Jules!

Noel   Martin wasn't too happy. I think he's getting a bit old for his granny.

Noel *opens the wine crate.*

June *goes into the kitchen and turns on the kitchen light. Doesn't see* **Julian** *slumped at the table.*

May   He'll be fine. You got wine?

Noel   Tucks of it.

June *goes to the counter and opens the bag. Takes out a cake box and a little bag of meat.*

June   Good God, what is this?

Julian   It's a bombe.

June   Ah!

May   Oh! What about my fags?

Noel   As requested.

Julian   Pineapple ice cream stuffed with rum-soaked ginger biscuits –

May   And fresh cream?

Noel *hesitates.*

June *takes the luscious dessert out of the box.*

Julian   – covered in toasted walnuts.

May   Well?

June   What are you doing sitting in the dark –?

Julian   It's called Castro's Bombe.

Noel   Fuck, fuck, fuck!

Julian   Oh God.

Noel *enters his kitchen.*

Noel   Do we really need cream?

May   Yes, for the main course and the dessert.

Julian   It's too much – a monumental balls-up.

Noel   Sure, none of us will bother with dessert.

May   Maybe, but you have to serve it anyway.

Noel   A bit of fruit. Make custard?

Julian   I want to throw up.

May   Ah, Noel, it's you keep going on about not letting ourselves down in front of this English couple.

Julian   Fuck!

Noel   Fuck!

Julian   Fuck!

Noel   Fuck!

June   Get a hold of yourself.

May   And Darina's coq. I need double cream for that.

Julian (*points at newspaper*)   Look.

Noel   Right, right, okay, okay. Spa here will go and roam the streets for cream.

Noel *exits to dining room. Takes out a bottle of wine from the crate. Gets a corkscrew.* **May** *continues cooking.*

June (*reads*)   'Last of the Summers Wine' – oh Christ.

Julian   Yes.

June (*reads*)   'Not only has the whiff of sleaze taken poor Julian and June Summers off the guest lists at New Labour shindigs these days, but the diary hears that their favourite Jermyn St. wine merchant' – oh Christ – 'has just cancelled their account.'

Julian   Fucking Guardian bastards.

June (*reads*)   'Does the vengeance of New Labour have no limits? Does upsetting the Party elite now mean you can't even get a decent drink in the Westminster area . . .' Oh Julian.

Julian   It's my fault. I'm an awesome galactic fuck-up.

June   I told you not to read this tripe.

Julian   I'm a freak show.

June   Another panic attack?

Julian   Yes.

June   Where this time?

Julian   I was in Sainsbury's –

June   Oh not in Sainsbury's.

Julian   Yes. At the meat counter. I panicked. Lost it. It was like I stuck my foot out in the box without meaning to; man down, penalty, red card, world crashing in . . . and I just couldn't . . . I – I ended up with that –

Waves towards the packages.

Noel *pours two glasses of wine. Drinks one and pours again.*

June   Castro's bombe, and . . . ?

Julian   Premium mince.

June   Minced beef – for the dinner party?

Julian   Call me Ishmael. I just pointed. That's what he gave me. Sorry June.

June   Why didn't you go somewhere quiet to calm down and –

Julian   I tried. I threw up.

June   In Sainsbury's?

Julian   Angel Underground.

June   Oh good, not our station. Right then, problem: what to do for a dinner party with minced beef and a cream mountain.

Julian   I'll check Jamie Oliver.

June   He's not answering our calls either. Solpadeine?

Julian   Please.

June *puts the bombe in the freezer and gets some water and Solpadeine for* **Julian**.

Noel *re-enters kitchen with bottle of wine and glasses.*

May   I thought you'd gone out to get –

Noel   I'm going. I'm going. Have a taste. South African.

May   South African? – is that all right?

Julian   It's complete crap, this is so –

June (*massages his shoulders*)   Relax relax relax.

Noel   Arthur in the off-licence said they're going wild for it in London at the moment. Something to do with your man Mandela.

May   Is it very dear?

Noel   Of course it's dear. Do you think these people won't know if we've been mangy with the wine?

June   Actually, have we got enough wine?

She rushes off to check. **Julian** *buries his face in his hands.*

> **May**   I'm only saying when you don't know if it's nice or not –
>
> **Noel**   Jesus, if it's good enough for Mandela. Anyway, don't worry. I only got six South African. I got that very dear Spanish one, mmm, nice tho', two French, two Australian, that Californian you like, and ah . . . something from Chile.
>
> **May**   Thirteen bottles?
>
> **Noel**   One free with every twelve.

June   Six bottles.

> **May**   But there's only four of us.
>
> **Noel**   We'd better get moving so.
>
> *He drinks and pours another.*

June   And some gin, and whiskey.

> **May**   Ah, Noel. Why won't you –
>
> **Noel**   Just testing the South African. Make sure it's not shite.
>
> **May** *sighs, goes to the dining room to fix the table settings.* **Noel** *brings the crate of wine to the kitchen. Still drinking.*

June   We'll survive – I think.

Julian   Even with him?

June   God yes, he could knock it back couldn't he?

Julian   Yes – Oh, Christ – flashback. June, can I just say something?

June (*checking watch*)   Make it quick. They're due in half an hour.

Julian (*looks horrified*)   It's okay, forget it.

June   Any inspiration from Jamie?

Julian   Not yet. Darling does this have to be tonight?

June   Sorry?

Julian   This . . . tonight. Do we have to?

June   Yes. They're only in London for some Michael Flatley premiere tomorrow.

Julian   Michael Flatley? Is he still alive?

June   Must be, he's having a premiere.

May   Is this an important night, love?

Julian   I suppose.

Noel   What do you think?

June   Some big Irish 'aren't we great we're all so rich' knees-up.

May   I'm just saying if so – shouldn't we, you know –

June   Seize the moment I say.

May   Really make an effort.

June   The chance may not come again.

Noel   Ah, shut up, will you.

Julian   Okay, okay, yes, okay.

June   Anyway, don't worry about the food. If I remember correctly he'd eat anything.

Julian   That's certainly how I remember him.

June *goes into the dining room. The two women criss-cross each other setting the same table. Funny business with cutlery.*

Julian   Right, right, okay. Jules do your stuff. Something quick, something not too subtle. As I remember, the old soak had a palate like a stray dog, so anything cheesy, garlicky, oh, and heavy on the booze – of course.

June   Didn't he have a particular thing for South African wine?

Noel (*drinking*)   This is great stuff. They'll be impressed with this.

Julian   Christ, yes. Thought it was the dog's bollocks for some reason.

Noel   I mean, apart from it being the 'in' thing in London. It's tasty.

June   God, South African wine; that was so last century.

Noel   We're on a winner here, honey bunch.

Julian   Should we try get some just for him?

June   No time, darling.

May   Noel, I really need that cream soon. I've softened the onions and garlic, the bacon is seared –

June   Anyway, he'll have moved on.

Noel   I'm just having a sip.

June   You know, Norwegian wine –

Julian   – Greenland wine.

They laugh.

May   It's just that Super-valu will be closed –

June   And it's so late already –

Noel   Will you fuck off and stop nagging?

Julian (*moan*)   Oooh.

June   Are you upset?

Noel   Over a bit of cream?

June *goes back into the kitchen.*

June   What is it?

Julian *moans head on the table.*

Noel   Fuckin' cream.

Julian   Oh sweet Christ.

Noel   Sweet Christ, fuckin' cream!

Julian   It's making me nauseous.

June   Darling.

Noel   What do you think I am, ha?

Julian   Such an awesome prat, I know.

Noel   Ha?

June   Count to ten.

Noel   Your slave, is that it?

June   Take a breath.

Noel   Running around for you.

June   Nice and slow.

Julian *goes to* **June**.

May *goes to* **Noel**.

May   Noel, go and get the cream now and get it over with. All right? Sorry and all that –

June   Look. I know it's so awful we have to do this.

May   – But it has to be done.

June   We haven't any choices. You've seen the latest demand?

Noel   Point taken. I'm gone. Out the door.

Julian   Well, that's just a joke.

June   They're not joking.

May   Remember, double cream. I know it's dearer –

June   Nine hundred thousand pounds.

May   But it's worth it.

June   And they intend to get it from us. But they won't.

Julian   You're incredibly strong.

Noel   You're a great woman, May, do you know that? I mean it.

Julian   I don't know what I'd do without you.

May   Grand – now will you get the cream.

June   Tonight will probably be horrible. But look, just keep thinking, this old Irish pig may save our bacon.

Noel *exits.* **May** *goes to her worktop and continues preparing the meal. There are chicken fillets to be sliced up.*

Julian   Right, yes, fine.

June   And anyway who else is there? We have no friends left.

Julian   Oh that's not true.

June   None with money or influence.

Julian   Ah.

June   They're all on-message it seems, and the message is, sorry not available to take your calls. Now focus.

Julian   Yes. Okay. Fully frighteningly focussed. As focussed as fuck.

June (*checks watch*)   Good.

Julian   What have we got? What have we got to compliment *Le boeuf haché*?

He rummages as **May** *slices* *and* **June** *sets.*

Julian   Peppers . . . broccoli . . . excellent, some red onions . . .

June   What did she like, can you remember?

> **May** *reads aloud from a cookbook as she prepares.*
>
> **May**   . . . strips of free-range chicken seared on a very hot pan . . .

Julian   His wife? I don't know. She was sort of Mousy, Wifey, Irishy.

June   She was decent.

Julian   Was she?

June   She was probably the real reason we did him that very large favour.

Julian   We made him.

> **May**   Very very rich. But don't worry yourself . . .

Julian   When I think of what we did. After what he did.

> **May**   Don't feel guilty . . .

Julian   Christ I need a drink?

> **May**   '. . . make it a good-sized mug of dry white wine.' Ah sure what the hell.

June   Jules. Jules. Jules. Focus on the job in hand. What have you dreamed up? Burgers and chips?

Julian   What an excellent idea. Or shepherd's pie. Doesn't Marco have it on his menu now? If it's good enough for him –

June   Just think big. Big fat Irish portions. To soak up the booze.

Julian   Meatballs. I see meatballs . . . .

June   You think?

Julian   Actually yes. Spicy meatballs.

June   There, I'm sure it'll be fine. Good. Now. Panic over?

Julian   Hm? Yes.

June   Sure?

Julian   I'm centred as fuck.

June (*checks watch*)   We've twenty minutes. Just enough time.

> **May**   For best flavour, let it all reduce . . .

Julian   I mean he owes us doesn't he? It shouldn't be a problem.

> **May**   Be particularly careful . . .

June   I should certainly hope he remembers –

> **May**   . . . not to be in any hurry . . .

June   It was thanks to us –

> **May**   Adding the stock.

Julian   I know –

June   – that his stock rose in the first place.

> **May** *continues cooking.*

Julian and **June** *prepare the meatballs and vegetables.*

Julian   And look at him now.

June   Even getting a message to him felt like a sort of privilege.

Julian   The extraordinary nerve of him not to speak to you directly. I mean, having you lurk in a hotel lobby while flunkeys and runners pass messages up and down. Who the fuck does he think he is. Paddy O'Brunei?

June   Look. It's not who he is, it's who he thinks we are.

Julian   Did he not remember us? Will you slice these?

June   Yes, of course he does, that's the point I'm making. How small?

Julian   Slivers.

June   We are the past. We are his low point.

Julian   The feeling is entirely mutual.

June   Nobody wants to remember being a beggar.

Julian   So why is he coming?

June   Who knows. My humble petition went up. The reply came back. Granted. He's coming tonight. Let's just be grateful. That okay? (*The peppers.*)

Julian   Perfect.

June   We must judge our approach very carefully.

Julian   Right, yes. He probably knows we're drowning in shit.

June   Of course he does. He'll enjoy that, so stay calm.

Julian   Calm as fuck.

June   Let him have his fun. What's really important is the language we use. Nothing too direct or straightforward, but neither can we sound opaque. He'll think we're trying to pull one over on him. We have to make sure he knows our proposal is illegal but we can't imply we think he's dodgy. Be friendly obviously but not presumptuous. Never come on like we're old pals. Keep away from potentially difficult topics, Irish history, Irish Culture, Irish music, Irish sport. In fact if we can avoid mentioning Ireland at all . . . Julian.

Julian   Hm, oh sorry, yes. Sorry I was – the meatballs.

June   Jules. Look at me. You'll be all right won't you? I need you on top form tonight.

Julian   Yes. Yes. Yes.

June   So, what sort of small talk will, you know, keep us ontrack?

Julian   Well . . . we don't want to say anything to antagonise him, bearing in mind the last time – I mean I know that was then –

June   But we have to have some conversation. It can't be all nods, winks, say no more.

Julian   I can see that.

June   So, any suggestions?

Julian   To be honest . . . right. Totally totally honest. That night had a strange effect on me. Not good. Bit of a red mist. Bit of the drunken nutter on the bus roaring in my face sort of vibe. That's the actual truth June.

June   There is no one else willing to help us. No one. And yes I know he had a lot of that old I hate the English stuff, but it was only . . . that's it . . . Jules you're a genius. We can turn all that crap to advantage.

Julian   We can?

June   Yes. What if . . . what if . . . we make him believe he's helping us pull off a fantastic scam against the Government, against the Queen herself practically.

Julian   You think?

June   Of course. Tax dodging is in his blood anyway. Tax dodging the Queen would be practically a religious thing.

Julian   Yes. I see. Okay. Chilli oil or chilli powder?

June   And don't forget – oil – he knows that we know where at least some of his bodies are buried.

Julian   That's true.

June   Which I suspect is probably why he's agreed to come here.

Julian   You're right.

June   Not that such a thing would ever be mentioned of course.

Julian   No. But it could hover in the air. I mean that tribunal in Dublin a couple of years back. Land deals, backhanders, he was up to his bollocks in it.

June   He got away with it though.

> **Noel** *enters to dining room.*

Julian   It's Ireland, darling.

June   But we have the kind of evidence that might ruin him even in Ireland.

Julian   You think?

June   No probably not. Which of course is why Ireland is the place for us. No one here will bail us out. What's the alternative?

Julian   Bankruptcy, gaol.

June   Unless we find a third way.

Julian   Christ if we could. Injury time; a Beckham free kick, top corner – yes!

June   There you go. (*The onions and garlic chopped.*)

> **Noel** *enters kitchen.*

Julian   Okay, I'll face him. Let's do it. What do you think? Balls big enough?

He holds up a prototype meatball. **June** *sighs.*

> **Noel** *holds up a tiny carton of cream.*
>
> **Noel**   Biggest they had, I'm afraid.
>
> **May**   Oh, Noel, that's no good.
>
> **Noel**   So I got you ten of them. (*Produces bag.*) Enough cream for dessert, for the main course, for your corn flakes in the morning, and maybe for a few brandy Alexanders later on tonight if the mood is right. (*A bottle of Remy Martin.*) Remy Martin.

May   Ah, not more drink.

Noel (*outrageous French*)   Rrrremeee Marrrrtang! That should impress the Brits.

May   I'm sure. Get out of my way now, while I do this.

Noel   Do you know what? I've a good feeling about tonight.

Julian   I still have a bad feeling about tonight.

Noel *goes into the dining room.*

May   It'll be grand.

June   Look. Be sensible and focus on the end result. It'll be painless. (*Checks watch.*) Fifteen minutes.

June *also goes into the dining room and continues dressing the table, while* **Noel** *sits there messing with arrangements.* **Julian** *continues making meatballs.*

May   Although why you have to wine and dine some English fellah just for a loan –

Noel   It's complicated, May.

May   Surely any of the banks here will give you a loan.

Noel   Of course they would.

May   Your credit is good, isn't it?

Noel   Don't worry yourself about it.

May   Especially after those fabulous apartments you built out by the canal. Sure you sold the lot off the plans didn't you?

Noel   We did all right.

May   Our retirement secured, you told me.

Noel (*to himself*)   Jesus, does she ever – (*Loud.*) Yes.

May   – and that offshore thing, whatever it is.

Noel   This has nothing to do with that. This is something else.

May   But what I'm saying is can't you bring all that money onshore again and use it. I mean better than getting a loan and paying big interest to some English fellah. And what if you get done on the sterling, then you'd be ragin' –

Noel *goes to the kitchen.*

Noel   May, May, May –

May   What?

Noel   You know fuck all about money matters. You're giving me a headache.

May   Sorry.

Noel   What's up with you? Normally you don't bother your head about any of this, now suddenly you're like a tax inspector smelling a rat.

May   I'm sorry love.

June   Right, I'll go and change then shall I?

Noel   Why I don't know. Is there something on your mind?

Julian   Something sexy I hope.

May   A small thing.

Julian   Something revealing.

Noel   Spit it out –

June   Do my best.

Noel   You know me May. In life and in business, straight as a die.

Julian   But with an air of mystery. Enigmatic, sensual.

June *exits and* **Julian** *continues preparing the food during this:*

May   Well . . . it's just. I don't say anything normally because I understand you have to do your things your way.

Noel   That's right.

May   And I know that as a person, as the person I know, you're as honest as the next man, but of course in this country it's not what you know, as much as who you know.

Noel   As much as who you know, that's the point May –

May   – So you have to keep well in with people like that Minister pal of yours and the funny looking fellah down in the corporation for the planning and councillors of course all sorts even your man who goes to gaol for a week here and a week there. That's all fine –

Noel   You're thinking about the tribunal aren't you? That's what's on your mind isn't it?

May   Well . . .

Noel   What am I being asked to do May?

May   I don't know really . . . ahm . . .

Noel   You saw the letter they sent. What am I being asked to do?

May   Help them –

Noel   What were the words?

May   Clarify some matters, they said –

Noel   Yes. Exactly. No accusations of any kind. I explained this to you. Put it out of your mind 'cause at the rate they're going it'll be 18 months or two years before they even get round to me. They might never. I'm small fry. I'm a nobody. Some old fucking builder.

May   Oh, I know, sure –

Noel   So that's gone, is it?

May   Right.

Noel Out of your head completely?

May Yes.

Noel Good. (*Pours another drink.*)

May I mean I suppose it's just I'm confused.

Noel *sighs.*

May No you see wait – no, 'cause . . . there's never been anyone from England visiting before. The only time you ever even mention England is about when you were there working on the sites years ago, and that's only stories about yourself and the lads and things you got up to, hijinks and so on and the awful things you had to put up with from snobby English –

Noel May, is all this leading somewhere, or is it complete shite-talk?

May Well all I'm saying is . . . you're trying to get that shopping centre built.

Noel I know what I'm trying to do.

May That's the big thing for you at the moment. And I mean it sounds just fabulous now, a great amenity, if you can get it going. So this Englishman – what has he to do with it? You know, I was just wondering . . .

Noel What does be going on in your head at all?

May Nothing. I mean –

Noel You're worried that something I'm doing might turn out to be a bit illegal maybe? Hm?

May No, no, no . . .

Noel Do you think so little of me?

May Ah Noel. I just prefer it when it's clear in my head what the thing is.

Noel (*sighs*)   Julian Summer was referred to me by the Minister personally – does that ease your mind?

May   Was he?

Noel   This fellah, he actually hires the Minister, the Minister works for him in other words, as a consultant on any issues related to his business and Ireland.

May   Go way.

Noel   Oh yes. Holds him in high esteem. So if he thinks I should meet this Mr Summers, I'm not going to say no am I?

May   No, of course not.

Noel   A hello session. Contacts May.

May   Right. But you mentioned a loan –

Noel   That's only – that's nothing – that's only to give us a talking point.

May   So this really has nothing to do with the planning permission for the shopping centre?

Noel   What made you think it had?

May   Just, I suppose that's what's taking up all your time at the moment, and then suddenly you invite this Englishman over –

Noel (*sighs*)   May, love . . .

May   Yes?

Noel   Is that something burning?

May   Oh Jesus.

Noel   I'll open a few more of these. Let them breathe.

May *saves the food, while* **Noel** *opens more bottles of wine. Drinking fairly continuously.*

Noel   The thing is to relax May, tonight is just a bit of plain simple Irish hospitality. 'Course now just because I might want to do business with this fellah whenever, whatever, doesn't mean we have to lick his hole either.

May (*the rice*)   I think it'll be all right.

Noel   I haven't met him, mind you. He might be sound as a trout, but you know what the English are like generally. If they think they have the upper hand at all then you might as well just curl up in a corner and wave the white flag.

Julian *in the dining room, knocks over wine.*

Julian   Oh blue bollocks.

Noel   They just can't help themselves putting the boot in. Grind down the small man. They just think they're naturally superior . . . That's the class system for you. You see we don't have any of that shite –

Julian *is now on his hands and knees furiously wiping up.*

Noel *is standing over him. Drinking.*

Noel   One man's as good as another over here. No distinctions. Not like the Brits. So the thing I learned over the years is, never look like you need them. Stand up to them. Eyeball to eyeball and never blink.

May   I hope they're on time, dinner should be ready in about fifteen minutes.

Noel   If they're late it's their fault. Make them apologise.

May   Ah can't we just have a nice civilised evening.

Noel   After what they did to this country?

May   What? – Oh, Noel, I thought you wanted to get on with this man.

Noel   On my terms. Not on his terms. A good kick up the hole is what they need sometimes.

As **Noel** *kicks,* **Julian** *moves away just in time, throwing down the cloth in despair, like a distressed child.*

Julian   Christ, I feel like I'm third class on the *Titanic*. June!

May   What's his wife's name?

Noel   Haven't a clue.

Julian   June!

Noel   Who cares.

Julian   Please!

May   It's just sometimes you get an idea of someone's personality from their name.

Julian   June!

Noel   What's her personality got to do with it? Just be nice to her.

May   Of course I will. What else would I be?

Noel   Well, I don't want you messing everything up –

May   Ah, Noel!

Noel   By saying the wrong thing, some stupid thing.

Julian   For Christ's sake!

Noel   She's probably a lady –

May   I'm sure she is.

Noel   – and English women are very sensitive when they're ladies.

June *reappears, looking quite stunning.*

June   I'm not fucking deaf.

May   I'm sure she'll be gorgeous.

Noel   Doesn't matter if she's ugly as Mick Moore's wife – you'll still be nice to her.

June   Oh no.

May   Of course I will. – She'll never be as ugly as poor Mick's wife, will she?

Julian   Sorry.

May   Poor thing –

June   Not now. Please.

Noel   No I'm sure his bird'll be a fine looking woman. Just leave her with a good impression.

June   This is such wrong timing –

Noel   Make her happy.

June   I get so angry.

May   Don't worry.

Julian   Sorry.

June   Not with you. With myself.

Noel   And are you going to clean yourself up at all?

Julian   Such a mess.

May   Well – I'd love to. Can you keep an eye on the food. You know without –

Julian   Knocking stuff over. So stupid.

Noel   Will you relax?

June   I feel so useless.

Noel   Go on, doll yourself up, they'll be here soon.

May *exits.* **Noel** *drinks and pointlessly stirs food. The more he gets bored the faster he will drink.*

June   I should be able to help you see sense but I can't. It's my fault, a complete failure to communicate, which has left you cut adrift.

Julian   No, it's me, I'm being hysterical. You're fantastic.

June leads **Julian** *to the sofa and pours him a drink. Massages his shoulders as they talk.*

June   Look. Let's understand this clearly. I know it must seem to you I've been barging ahead, making plans, not keeping you up to speed and this is the result. Breakdown. I'm really sorry. It's just there genuinely is so little time. (*Checks watch.*) Ten minutes in fact.

Julian   Why is he coming? What is he up to?

June   How do you mean?

Julian   When you suggested contacting him. I didn't believe he'd come.

June   Fair enough. But why would he bother to come unless he's well-disposed towards you?

Noel (*sneering*)   Mmm – cheers, old chap.

Julian   I suppose.

Noel   Old sport.

Julian   That's what I've been trying to tell myself. So I kept my mouth shut.

June   Kept your mouth shut? You said it was a great idea.

Julian   I probably gave that general impression, yes.

Noel   You smart-alec fuck.

June   No. You said, go ahead, contact him.

Julian   True. But you see . . . I never thought he'd say yes. I thought he'd think . . .

Noel   English bollocks.

Julian   . . . it was a bad idea. Like me.

June   Like you?

Julian   Yes. The truth is . . . the real truth is . . . I don't want to meet him.

Noel   He'd better not make me beg –

June   Oh come on!

Julian   No, really. I'd rather not.

Noel   If he makes me beg –

June   But we did him a big favour.

Noel *chuckles dangerously.*

Julian   Exactly.

Noel   Thanks for the cash, now fuck off back to England.

June   This is all news to me Jules – darling.

Julian   I know. I'm sorry.

June   I mean he wasn't the most pleasant man I've ever met by a long long way. But no worse than some of those Bulgarians or Latvians surely.

Julian   No he's different. They're just crims. He doesn't work that way. I think he's motivated by some horrible negative . . . primal thing. Remember, he needed a favour from us.

June   And we gave it to him.

Julian   And I think it made him hate us more.

June   That was then. But he's become so fabulously successful he must have changed.

Julian   He's over here to see Michael Flatley?

June   Fair point.

Noel   May, how often do I have to stir this shite?

May (*off*)   Constantly.

Noel *continues drinking and stirring.*

June   So it's this that's brought back the panic attacks, not the newspaper stuff.

Julian   Yes.

June   But it was one night when? . . . five – six years ago.

Julian   I know.

June   I mean, okay, he was too much, but wasn't he just – being Irish?

Julian   Yes, well I'd never had someone be Irish all over me before.

June   Was it like when I first met your parents?

Julian   Right, at least you know the feeling.

June   But six years later, I had gotten used to it?

Julian   Oh come on darling, my parents may not have been as friendly as one would like –

June   I didn't wake up screaming and sweating anymore.

Julian   Do you not remember how gruesome as fuck that night was.

June   Well God knows we've had a few gruesome nights.

Julian   For sure.

June   And we've been to Dublin several times since then.

Julian   Not for a couple of years.

June   I know, but we have been there since that night –

Julian   Only when he wasn't there.

June   – We like Dublin – What?

Julian   Only when I was sure he wasn't around.

June   How could you be –

Julian   I used to check.

Pause.

Noel *tastes the sauce.*

> **Noel** Mmm – bit more of the vino I think.
>
> *He pours in a lot of wine.*

June Jules darling. Take me through this.

> **Noel** Some for you, some for me.

Julian Well you know how everyone knows everyone's business in Dublin?

June Keep going.

Julian So . . . well . . . whenever you suggested a trip over, weekend break or whatever, I'd get on the phone to people I knew there to try and check out what his movements were. If he was going to be away, then I'd feel it was safe to go. But if he was around – well Dublin's pretty small and I wouldn't really be comfortable knowing we might bump into him –

June You've never told me anything about this.

Julian Well of course not – you'd think I was lunar module, lost in space.

June Yes I would.

Julian There you are.

June (*checking her watch*) I really am trying to get my head round this.

> **Noel** *enters dining room, drinking.*

Julian Okay. August weekend three years ago. I got sick suddenly and we had to cancel.

June The mystery virus.

Julian I had been assured he was going to be in his new villa in the Algarve that weekend, but then the night before we travelled, I got a call from one of my contacts on the ground –

June Contacts on the ground?

Noel *sits between* **Julian** *and* **June**.

Julian   – to say that he'd been spotted drinking in the Shelbourne. The family was gone, but he was still around.

June   Julian –

Julian   I know I know –

June   Contacts on the ground? You're not suddenly going to reveal that you work for MI5 are you?

Julian   No. Why would I do that?

June   Then what was all that about?

Noel   Looks, if I see him giving me any of those looks.

Julian   I just couldn't face it. I couldn't take the chance on bumping into him.

June   But why?

Noel   Looking down on me.

Julian   I keep telling you I'm . . . nervous I suppose.

June   Yes?

Julian   More than that obviously. Tense. Yes, tense and nervous. But that doesn't quite . . . capture it either . . .

Noel   So what? Am I supposed to be afraid like?

June   Are you afraid?

Noel   Afraid I'll get my walking papers?

Julian   I mean the word is not entirely inaccurate – I know it seems like a such a silly word, but you know. In a certain way . . .

Noel   No empire any more.

June   Darling, darling honestly I understand, okay, really, really. But aren't you just – what? – disgusted by him perhaps or bored by his incessant –

Julian   All right all right, so afraid isn't really the word for it . . . whatever.

Noel   No culture. Nothing.

June   Let's be sensible. Tell me honestly. Is there something else I should know?

Noel *chuckles dangerously.*

Julian   No.

June   Honestly?

Julian   I met him that one night. We met him. We did him that favour. That's it.

Noel   Nothing, only tabloids and hooligans.

June   So? We really have very little time.

Julian   Don't you think there was something psychotic about him?

June   You think he's going to kill you?

Julian   No of course not. Not in that way. How can I put it?

Noel *is by now quite pissed. The demons are well out. Sings.*

Noel   'British soldiers tortured Barry just because he would not tell . . .' (*Sings on over next speech.*)

Julian   Ok. It's like this. I get the chance to play in the Champions League final right? Fantastic. But as I go out on the pitch at the San Siro, I'm told that I'm man-marking Roy Keane.

Noel (*sings*)   'Turn informer or we'll kill you'

Julian   Ooooh! I feel these little prickles of – I don't know, okay so it's not fear but it's very very like fear.

Noel   Think we'll bow the knee do you?

Julian   It's a deep deep dread.

Noel   Like fuck.

Julian   A kind of Greek thing. Fate and stuff. Even before
I open my big mouth, I know, I know for sure that anything
I say will be a fuck up.

Noel   English fuck. You owe us remember. Big time.

Julian   Try a compliment, wrong! Patronising. Honest
criticism? Wooah wrong! Arrogant. How about a little joke?
No sorry. Being Superior. Like you said earlier, comment
on Ireland or anything Irish, I'm just showing my
ignorance. Don't mention Ireland at all? So insensitive.

Noel (*chant*)   'You'll ne-ver beat the Irish!'

June   Ignore all that. Move on.

Julian   I've tried. I can't. I thought I could and then you
suggested this thing, and it all came back. It's like a horrible
endless dance with two lunatic partners doing different
steps. If I said 'Oh look, it's raining,' he'd not only step out
and check, but even as he stood there getting soaked he'd
shrug as though in some more profound way my
observation had not been proven. If I said black, he
wouldn't say white, he'd say what did I mean exactly by
black. And my explanation of black would turn to ashes in
my mouth. Lame and unconvincing. And this is someone
who was asking me to do him a favour!

Noel   And don't give me that fucking hoighty toity look.

June   I'm beginning to see your point. In a completely
insane way of course. But I'm travelling with you.

Julian   So by the end of that . . . that awful night, I knew I
could never face even the possibility of meeting him again. I
know it's pathetic as fuck –

June   Look. You should have told me all of this at the
start. Or after I told you he had accepted our invitation, or
at any time before now.

Julian   I know.

June   So why didn't you?

Julian   Confront your demons I suppose.

June   Sorry?

Julian   My Dad was always saying things like that to me. 'There is no fear so terrible as the fear that is afraid to confront fear.'

June   Oh please . . .

Julian   Well you know that generation. Fed on Churchill.

June   The war didn't just release millions of people from the yoke of oppression. It released millions of cliches from the yoke of irony.

Julian   Anyway. I suddenly thought, 'Who dares wins?'

June   As I say . . .

Julian   If I can confront this fear, and win through, then I will succeed like I've never succeeded before.

June   All because your father spoke gibberish to you. – Cue panic attack in Sainsbury's –

Julian   I know I know I know I know. It's all bollocks. But I didn't want to let you down.

June   Well okay, let's be positive. If your Dad's, ah, philosophy helps you get through tonight –

Julian   No. I don't want to meet him. I can't.

June   Julian listen –

Julian   Let's cancel. What time is it?

June (*checks watch*)   They're due in less than 5 minutes.

Julian *starts a low moan. Rocking.*

June   You're not really your father's son are you.

Julian   No.

32   That Was Then

June   Thank Christ for that. Hate to be married to anything resembling that old bore.

June *embraces him, kisses his neck.*

May *appears resplendent.*

May   What do you think?

Julian   It's really scary.

June   No, it's just something unpleasant we have to put up with for a couple of hours.

Noel   Look at you . . . look at you. What'll you have?

May   Oh Noel. You're hammered already.

Noel   Jesus don't start.

May   Did you keep an eye on the dinner?

June   Look everything's prepared.

Noel   Relax.

June   Meatballs –

May   Thank God.

June   Peppers –

Noel   Smell that.

June   Garlic, Onions

May (*tastes*)   Ooooh!

June   Chilli oil

May   Too much wine. How did that –

June   Tomatoes.

Julian   Okay.

Noel   So come on. Have a drink with me.

June (*checks watch*)   I'll do those. Get ready.

Julian *exits.*

> **May**   Still it tastes nice.
>
> **Noel**   So what's the puss on you for?
>
> **May**   I'm making you coffee. I just don't see how you're going to make any kind of impression on this man in that state.
>
> **Noel**   What? We'll have a laugh. Let him take us as he finds us.
>
> **May**   Even if he finds you under the table.
>
> **Noel**   Ah stop being an old moan. Have a sup.
>
> **May**   Well – a little taste before the meal.
>
> **Noel**   That's my girl.
>
> *Pours.*
>
> **May**   I mean I don't mind you getting drunk pet. You know that. I just hate you being drunk before the guests even get here. You'll have the coffee?
>
> **Noel**   Maybe I will – just for you. You're looking gorgeous do you know that.
>
> **May**   Thanks.
>
> **Noel**   May, May, my little early summer flower.
>
> **May**   Ah Noel.
>
> **Noel** (*sings*)   'Queen of the angels. Queen of the May . . .'
>
> *They laugh and embrace and kiss. It is surprisingly tender.*

Julian *returns, dressed for dinner.*

June   Feeling any better?

Julian   I think so – thanks.

> **Noel**   Do you know something? Whatever I paid for that gear, it was worth it.

June   Mmm, it actually tastes rather good.

> **Noel**   And I tell you something else. This English fuck better compliment you on your looks or he'll have to deal with me.

Julian   Oh. Have we an aperitif to offer them?

June   Rubbing alcohol?

They laugh. **June** *gets lemons and slices them.*

> **May**   Good strong coffee. There.
>
> **Noel**   You're a fabulous woman May – keeping me on the straight and narrow.
>
> **May**   Well I can only do my best – I suppose you have to get this money from the man don't you?
>
> **Noel**   Yeah, yeah, yeah.
>
> **May**   So I suppose if it has to be done . . .
>
> **Noel**   Best to have a clear head. I know that.
>
> **May**   And be nice.
>
> **Noel**   Course I will.
>
> **May**   I mean if the Minister himself suggested you talk to him, it probably means he's respectable anyway.
>
> **Noel**   Oh he's sound. I've been assured of that.

June   A couple of g and t's, nice food, a relaxed atmosphere . . .

Julian   If only.

June   I'm telling you.

> **May**   And English people are very straight now, you have to say that for them, no matter how snobby they sound.

June   We'll end up chatting like old friends. A discreet mention of favours . . . He'll know the right thing to do.

May   By the end of the night, we'll be laughing.

June   Easy Peasy.

Julian/ **Noel**   Know what? You're absolutely right.

June (*checks watch*)   No panic. He's not the type to be on time anyway.

The buzzer buzzes.

May   It's them.

Julian   It's them!

May   On the dot.

June   Calm down.

Noel   I'll get it.

May   Stay right where you are.

June   Remember. Nothing to be afraid of.

Julian   I know. I know.

May *is struggling with* **Noel***. Buzzer again.*

May   Stay in the kitchen. You're in no condition –

June   Ready?

Noel   Of course I am.

Julian   Ready as I'll ever be.

Julian *and* **June** *go to open the door. Disappear briefly as*

Noel *and* **May** *struggle. Buzzer.*

Noel   I'm fighting fit.

May   Oh don't say that.

Noel *breaks free and opens the door.* **Julian** *and* **June** *standing on the other side wearing coats (hats?).*

Noel   Aha! You made it.

The **Julian** *who now arrives at* **Noel**'s *home is quite different to the one we've seen so far. He's confident. In fact rather arrogantly self-assured.* **June** *behaves very much the same.*

Julian   Noel Gregory? Master Builder and Entrepreneur at large?

Noel   That's me. Julian Summer?

Julian   And partner.

June   Are we on time?

May   Perfect.

Julian   This is –

Noel   And this is the bird ha. Nice going. Nice going Julian.

May   You're very welcome.

Julian   Thank you.

May   Hello. I'm May.

June   And I'm Ju – just delighted to meet you.

Julian   Delighted.

Noel   And does the little birdie have a name?

June   Sorry?

May   Noel, drinks. What'll you have?

Julian   Oh we're in Dublin. Guinness on tap surely.

May *takes their coats:*

May   Noel'll organise a drink.

May *exits.*

Noel   We've a – we got some (*Proudly.*) South African wine.

June   Oh . . . Lovely.

Noel   Got it in specially.

Noel *goes to get the wine.*

Buzzer.

Julian (*to* **June**)   It's going to be a great evening. Yeah, yeah, yeah?

June   Yes. Open up.

Buzzer again. He turns to open the door.

Noel   Amazing man that Mandela fellah. Loves his wine apparently.

Julian *opens the door.* **April** *is standing there. Surprise.*

April   Hi.

Julian   Hello – ah –

April   Hi, I'm April.

June   Sorry. You're looking for . . .

April   I'm with Noel. You're expecting us. He's just parking.

Julian   Oh. I see. Come in.

June   Yes please.

Noel *brings the wine.*

Noel   Now, Meerlust '96. Special Reserve.

June (*whisper*)   What's going on? Where's his wife?

Julian (*whisper*)   I don't know.

Noel *pouring wine.*

April   Actually, I came up first deliberately.

Noel   Now . . . here we go.

June   Thank you.

April   I know you haven't met Noel for some time.

> **Noel**   And for you, Julian.

April   You see – I'm Noel's new partner.

Julian (*to* **April**)   Great.

June (*to* **April**)   Great.

> **May** (*to* **Julian** *and* **June**)   Great.

April   We met each other at an AA meeting. My first one actually.

> **Noel** *clinks* **Julian**'s *glass.*
>
> **Noel**   Slainte. First of many.

April   A year ago. It's changed both our lives.

Julian/June   Fantastic!

> **May**   Now, dinner will only be about ten minutes everyone.
>
> **Julian/June**   Fantastic.

Buzzer. **June** *opens the door.* **Noel** *is there. This* **Noel** *is erect and sober.*

Noel   So hello Julian, June – I'm delighted. Something told me we were going to bump into each other again.

Blackout.

Act Two

A few minutes later in both time periods. For all of this act the two dinner parties are in progress simultaneously. Again when there is a sustained sequence in one area and time I have tried to give a general indication of what is happening elsewhere. It is important to remember that **Noel**, **Julian** *and* **June** *now exist in two different time periods and the performance and direction must signal clearly (and hopefully wittily and entertainingly) to the audience where they are at any one time.* **May** *and* **April** *will be of use here because of course* **May** *only exists in the past,* **April** *only in the future.*

Noel, **April** *and* **June** *are sitting at the dinner table.* **Julian** *is standing.* **May** *is in her kitchen tending to the food.*

Julian   Now supper's bubbling away. Pot luck really, so I hope you don't mind –

June   We've kept it very simple.

Julian   Yes . . . ah . . . very simple.

Sudden change to **Julian** *in Dublin. These switches will happen constantly throughout the rest of the play. Indicated by the direction: '(Switch.)'*

> Simple Irish fare. We're looking forward to it. What is it? Irish stew, Potato bread. All that.
>
> **June**   Julian loves Dublin.
>
> **Julian**   And how often do you get to the mainland?
>
> **Noel**   What's that?
>
> **Julian**   Of course I am assured the Guinness in London is like bogwater, so –

(Switch.)

– Happy to stick with ah . . . iced water.

April   We're fine, aren't we Noel?

Noel   Perfectly happy.

Julian   Actually we may have some – you know, what else have we darling? Do you take coke? – I mean drink ah cola.

April   Water is fine for me, but Noel you love a coke now and then don't you?

Noel   I enjoy one occasionally.

June   I'll get the starter then darling shall I?

Julian *looks at her puzzled. 'What starter?'*

June   You two re-acquaint yourselves after all this time.

She disappears. **Julian** *is very nervous.*

Julian   And ah . . . we have Ribena oh and I think some cranberry thing if you want to liven up the water a bit.

April   Really don't fuss. We're cool as we are.

Julian   Of course, of course.

April   We should probably have told you about Noel's new situation but he doesn't like to make a fuss about it, do you Noel?

Noel   It was a big step, but it's not something I want to carry like a badge everywhere I go. (*Switch.*)

Especially in front of important English folk over from the mainland, we have to put our best foot forward and lay on a bit of a do to impress you. May, what's keeping you?

May (*in kitchen*)   Won't be long pet.

Noel   Now music, music, have to have the bit of music. I know the very thing. Here we go . . .

He goes to the CD player. Turns on. Bob Marley's IS THIS LOVE begins. **Noel** *does little drunken moves back to the table.*

Julian   Nice moves young Noel. Very tasty. (*Switch.*)

June *returns with tapenade, tarragon oil and a plate of sliced bread.*

June   Black olive tapenade, tarragon oil and ah . . . some bread.

Julian (*embarrassed*)   Darling, it's Mother's Pride.

April   Sliced pan – excellent. Noel loves sliced pan.

Julian   Really?

Noel   Oh yes. You can't beat the old sliced pan.

Julian   Great – sliced pan – yes, I think people make a lot of fuss over tomato and fennel bread and walnut bread and all the rest, but as you say, three cheers for the good old sliced . . . pan.

June   Yes, it ah . . . lets the oil and the tapenade have their say.

April   Mmmm . . . mmmm. This is so civilised.

Julian   Music perhaps?

April   Oh yes please. Actually we have a bit of a special CD with us you might like to hear.

June   Lovely. What is it?

April   Six Teens. Their first album.

June   Sorry?

April   The boy band. They've had two number ones already.

Julian   Sixteens?

April   Isn't it clever? There's six of them you see and they're all teen-(agers) –

June   – Teenagers, yes, I see.

Julian   Six – Teens. Very good. And you're ah both fans?

April   I know them personally. And Noel's one of their backers.

Noel   An excellent investment so far.

Julian   Right, well we must hear the latest Irish boy band phenomenon. (*Switch.*)

Bob Marley sings on. **Noel** *still dancing.*

Julian   I have to say I thought you'd be more of a Daniel O'Donnell man.

Noel (*a look but says nothing*)   Did you now? Smoking Bob. Brings me back. Now sweetheart lovey – are you ready for a top up?

June   Happy as I am.

Julian   She hasn't got into the Dublin rhythm yet Noel.

Noel   You're going to have to keep up a faster pace than that tonight. 'I-I-I-I-I-I'm willing and able.' (*Fills* **Julian**'s *glass.*) Tell us. What does this remind me of?

Julian   Smoking ganja in the 70's?

Noel   Yeahyeahyeah oh course – but what thing exactly? A particular event. A moment in time.

May (*entering*)   Oh are you getting Bob Marley already? His wild London Summer.

Julian   Hammersmith 1975! Cheers.

Noel   Ah big mouth you gave it away.

May   Well I didn't know it was a state secret.

Noel   Ah what would you know. Let's drink to Bob and a summer night I'll never forget. (*Switch.*)

Except I can't recall who did the original version in the 70's. All I know is our lads have already sold twice as many copies, and it should break them into the US market. The big bucks.

June   Why don't we save this for later over coffee? When we can really listen properly.

April   Good idea. This kind of evening so suits Noel now.

Noel   Both of us.

April   In the past when he and his ex wife entertained, there was no intelligent conversation. It was all about drink.

Noel   Ah. It was very sad.

April   Everything was just an excuse for drink. Like food didn't really feature.

May   Sorry about the slight delay with the dinner.

Noel   We're fine, we're slugging away here.

May   Noel and I aren't ones for starters normally. So I hope you won't mind if we go straight for the main course.

Noel   Main course, ha? I keep telling her a few hang sandwiches would be grand, but she won't listen.

Noel *pours*.

May   You see what I have to put up with June. (*Switch.*)

April   Just drink, drink and more drink. She was so not good for him.

Noel   To be fair, she didn't intend any harm.

April   Essentially Noel's ex-wife was what we call an enabler. So . . . he had to get rid of her. (*Switch.*)

Noel   Will you go and get the grub woman, I'll look after the entertainment.

(*Switch.*) I'm afraid so. She was part of my drinking life. It was very sad but it had to happen. (*Switch.*)

'Is this love, is this love that I'm feeling.' And what May doesn't know is – you see I only met her the year after in Majorca – what she doesn't know is – I did the business with a young Jamaican one on the night of the concert. Oh Jasus! But ah I couldn't talk to her about that sort of stuff you know – she's a bit old fashioned that way. Not like you English girls, you're more out there yeah.

June   Oh we are, and as for those Jamaican girls –

> **Noel**   Don't be talking to me. (*Whispers.*) We did it four
> times. I was grand and fit from working on the sites. Happy
> days in old London town ha! (*Sings along.*)
>
> **Julian**   So are you sure there's not a young black Noel
> somewhere in Brixton, Guinness in one hand, Malibu in the
> other?
>
> **Noel**   Sure, what if there is – good luck to him.
>
> **June**   Julian, we've only just met Noel. (*Switch.*)

And suddenly here we all are after – how many years?

April   Well I wasn't around the last –

April *is already getting on* **June**'s *nerves*.

June   Yes, yes, I suppose I meant Noel and Julian and I
really.

Julian   You're looking very well Noel. Prosperity has done
you no harm at all.

June   No harm at all. It was very good of you to give up
your one free night to call round.

Noel   I felt I owed it to you.

Julian *and* **June** *exchange excited glances*.

Julian   Really? No.

April   Isn't the apartment lovely Noel?

June   Well thanks. I mean it's pretty much as we found it.

Noel   Rent sky high of course?

Julian   Absolutely. I mean it's –

June   How did you know we rented?

Noel   Oh . . . it's just . . . isn't that the way it is in an area
like this. From what I know of the London property market.

June   Well that's exactly right. But you might as well live
in a decent location.

Julian   If I remember correctly you were living in a beautiful part of Dublin.

Noel   Yes, it was very pleasant (*Switch.*)

Why? – what you were expecting? Pigs in the parlour right. The thatched roof falling in.

Julian   Steady on.

June   We were just complimenting your –

Noel   No, no, hold on now. I know this. I know this polite English act. Like the rest of us are fuckin eejits and as long as you have this kind of face on you – this supposed to be polite face – we won't know what you're really thinking. Now that might fool poor old May or someone – May! May! That might you know – but I spent too long on the sites in London dealing with your crowd.

May   Yes love?

Noel   Come here a minute. Look at this pair. Look at their faces.

May   Ah Noel now be nice. He's desperate sometimes but he doesn't mean it.

Noel (*switches off music*)   No, no, listen, now look at their faces would you, and tell us what you see.

May   Noel!

Noel   What do you fuckin' see?

May   I see two lovely nice people – who are getting very embarrassed at your antics.

Julian   We're rather enjoying the show actually.

June   It's all right really.

Julian   You're quite a character Noel.

May   Now how's that for a compliment. They think you're a character. (*To* **Julian** *and* **June**.) Ignore him. He's only showing off.

May *sits* **Noel** *down forcibly (Switch.) as* **May** *goes back to the kitchen.*

April   It was his quiet easy manner that attracted me wasn't it Noel?

Noel   I suppose you needed a calm presence in your life at that stage.

April   Still do. And confidence. Noel gave me confidence.

Noel   But you've really developed my cultural side honey. It was April introduced me to Flatley.

Julian   Oh yes, tomorrow night's the premiere is that right?

April   Well not just a premiere. It's a cultural phenomenon.

June   Do you think?

April   He's so talented. And inspirational.

Julian   I suppose . . .

June   He must have something special if you've taken so much trouble to come and see him Noel.

Noel   Well actually, I'm an investor in the show.

June   Oh.

Noel   Flatley might be getting on a bit now, but he still knows all about the colour of money.

Julian   More real than the colour of his hair, I hope.

Icy pause.

Noel   People who sneer at him like that usually wouldn't mind having his bank account.

June   Sorry, Julian didn't mean any –

Julian   Any slur. Truly. I'm sorry if you thought I was making fun of Irish people and red hair or anything like that.

Noel   What are you talking about?

Julian   Me? I don't know. Nonsense I suppose – you know.

June   Look – we might as well be clear about this. We were . . . concerned you might be sensitive to – you know – silly gibes about Irish people when that wasn't –

Noel   You were having a go at Flatley?

June   Not 'having a go' as such, it was just a silly remark which –

Noel   But sure Flatley isn't Irish, he's American.

Surprised pause.

Julian   Yes, yes, exactly, that's right. That's, that's exactly –

Noel   Of course he does the old Irish American act, but sure if that puts more dollars in the till, who's complaining?

Julian   I couldn't agree more. I have to . . . I have to . . . (*Switch.*)

I have to hand it to you Irish. That whole quaint charm act is such a great little scam. The Yanks fall for it all the time, don't they.

June   And now Europe as well.

Julian   Absolutely. Ireland is sort of the song and dance act on the Euro gravy train. Sing for your supper eh? Economic boom eh? (*He winks.*) Nice one.

June   While we poor stupid English keep paying the bills.

Noel   Why don't you just stand up on the table there.

June   Sorry?

Noel   No, go on. Stand up there on the table . . . so you can look down on me properly?

Julian   No you don't understand, we weren't –

Noel   Oh, I didn't understand – ah yeah, I'd be too thick for that.

June   No, we think you're smart –

Julian   Yeah, smart as fuck –

Noel   We put up with 800 years of this kind of thing, I don't have to put up with it now in my own house, with my poor missus slaving away in the kitchen –

May (*entering*)   Dinner is served.

Noel   – to feed you as well. Bring that back in.

May   What?

Noel   Bring it back into the kitchen, Jesus are you deaf? There'll be no food eaten in this house until they apologise.

Julian   Oh come on.

May   Ah Noel, what is it now?

Noel   I'll tell you what it is. The same old sneer. Oh yes, I remember it well myself, anything worthwhile the Irish get must be 'cause of some dirty deal or swindle but (*Switch.*)

you know we're all players on the world stage now, and once as a businessman you realise this, that technology has made geography irrelevant, Dublin – London – what does it matter then. (*Switch.*)

It drives me up the wall. It just makes me mad, that you can't accept in your heads that we are a free country, as good as you are –

Julian   You're way over the top my friend.

Noel   You see, you see – oh so patronising and superior

(*Switch*.) but you know something, our superiority won't last unless the Irish business community guards its advantage very closely. Britain could actually catch up very quickly if you went about it the right way. I mean we're very fortunate because thankfully being Irish really means something in the world. (*Switch*.)

It mightn't be much but I'm proud to be Irish and I'm fucked if I'm going to let people like you put me down. (*Switch*.)

The rising tide lifts all boats and right now the Irish are surfing the wave. It's very exhilarating.

April   Isn't it lovely to sit in a sober atmosphere, nibble tapenade and have intelligent conversation? (*Switch*.)

Noel   Fuckin' fucked up fucks and your fuckin' fuckology –

May   Noel, Noel love, the dinner will go cold very fast. I think maybe we all had a bit too much to drink without having had a bit of food inside us. Come on now, let's sit down and enjoy the meal. Go on . . . sit!

Noel *sits down.*

May   And I know there's things that you and Julian will want to talk about later, while June is giving me a hand with the dishes . . . Noel.

June *is about to say something sardonic, but in the circumstances thinks better of it. They wait for* **Noel** *to decide. He recollects his situation. Forced laugh.*

Noel   Had you going didn't I? Come on now I had. That was me having a laugh. Nothing personal, a bit of gas that's all. Grub's up folks. Are you hungry?

Julian   Not hugely.

May   It's a lovely recipe.

June   Yes May, I think some food would do us all good.

May   Darina Allen. She's on telly over here – she's fantastic. (*Switch.*)

Julian (*going to kitchen*)   Not quite Jamie Oliver standard I'm afraid, but it'll be okay.

May   I swear by Darina. (*Exits to kitchen.*)

June   He's learned everything he knows from TV chefs.

Noel   The power of television, ha?

April   It's amazing.

Julian and **May** *working in their respective kitchens.*

Noel   April works in television by the way.

June   Oh really – is that your job?

April   It is now. It's, like, totally changed my life. Before I was sober I used to work in PR. Well you know –

June   I can imagine, so tedious.

April   No, it was very exciting. I met so many interesting people, but . . . well the drink culture. And of course all free drink as well.

Noel   The worst kind.

June (*tiny irony*)   Of course. Awful.

April   It was my downfall. I knew I had to get out. So . . .

May   Sorry, the rice, a small problem.

April   I became a journalist with TV3.

May   A bit stuck together.

June   TV3?

May   Lumpy.

Noel   It's been going about five years now.

May   But I'll try and do something with it.

April (*proud*)   It's just become Ireland's most watched TV network with an audience share of over 34.8%

> **May** *in her kitchen is grappling with lumpen overcooked rice.*

Julian *is putting the meatballs into a serving dish.*

June   That must be exciting.

April   Working with TV3 helped me stop drinking.

June   And you're a journalist?

April   Yes. I'm the charity correspondent.

June   The ah – really?

Noel   It's a very popular segment.

April   I'm on every night as part of our investigative current affairs slot. A sort of charity round-up. Celebrity Breakfasts for Cerebral Palsy. Coffee Mornings for Cancer. Fashion Shows for Systic Fibrosis. I report on them all. There's always some fantastic charity event happening. Full of celebrities.

Noel   It was her own concept.

April   It's amazing how much people in Ireland give to charity. So uplifting. Ordinary people too, not just the celebs. I always try to feature ordinary people in the slot, 'cause you know you get tired of celebs all the time.

Noel   That's just us honey, because we have access to them all the time –

April   You're right, I shouldn't be blase.

Noel   For most of the viewers it's still a big thrill to see famous people give their money away.

April   It's such an exciting time in Ireland now. The success of TV3 is really a kind of symbol of our growing-up as a nation.

Noel   I'm certainly glad I invested in it.

April   But what about you? Noel told me you were very kind to him once, years ago.

June   Hmm – oh thank you Noel. Well I used to be an accountant I'm afraid.

Noel   Nothing wrong with that.

June   Oh sure, it was a living. Julian used to be ah . . . well, like yourself, a journalist. Nowhere near as glamorous of course; he was a foreign correspondent. He might have met the occasional celebrity terrorist but that was it really.

April   Sounds very interesting though.

June   Well actually it had its moments. He was right there when the wall fell in '89. That was a bit special.

April   Oh. Was he hurt?

June   Sorry?

April   You said a wall fell . . . ?

June   Ah . . . No, no, he wasn't hurt . . . but he did give up journalism soon after that.

April   Delayed shock probably –

June   Perhaps. Anyway he and I put our heads together and started a sort of specialist consultancy company.

Noel   They've helped a lot of people, honey.

June   Yes, especially politicians. They love the whole idea of consultancy. It sounds so important and yet is so wonderfully vague.

Noel   It's mainly introductions. The global handshake. Bringing people together for mutual benefit.

June   Yes, mutual benefit. That's the big thing. When we met Noel for example –

Noel (*a slight note of warning to* **June**)   That was then of course.

June   Of course – five years ago business was booming. But it's rather taken a turn for the worse at our end. As things have turned out, Julian and I are pretty well –

Julian *returns with dinner.*

Julian   Meatballs in a spicy sauce. Arrabiata to some but we'll call a spade a spade.

May *returns.*

May   Nearly there with the fragrant rice.

Julian   And rice.

May   Oh flip, I think the chicken might need a bit of a heat now?

May *picks up the chicken dish and*

Julian *puts the meatballs down in exactly the same place.*

Noel   Isn't it lucky I bought her the old microwave, hah. You big thick.

Julian   Now tuck in. Enough, ah, iced water folks?

Noel (*pouring more wine*)   Come on, you're too slow.

June   I think you're trying to get me pissed.

Noel   Meerlust '96 reserve. I'm told it'll be even better in six months time, but sure we can't wait that long.

Julian   We might have to if May doesn't win her battle with the rice. (*Calls.*) What do you say May?

Silence. **Julian** *knows he's made a terrible blunder.*

June   He was joking Noel.

Noel   Hm? Ah yeah, I know, sure.

June   He wasn't being –

Noel   Great jokers, the English.

Julian   Well, we like to think that we –

Noel   At other people's expense of course.

June   Oh Christ –

Noel   Is that what Cromwell said in Drogheda? Oh sorry, only joking lads.

Julian   Cromwell? What's Cromwell got to do with it?

Noel   That same face on him, all innocent, 'Only joking Pat.'

Julian   This is Cromwell?

Noel   Not Cromwell. We called him that. Can't remember his fucking name. Watching me like I'd be sciving off, if he as much as blinked.

Julian   I don't know what you're talking about.

Noel   You know well – remarks, English remarks. Even when the job is oxo, the little put down, 'Well glad to see the Guinness isn't affecting your work, Pat.' That's what he said to me one day – he actually said that the fucker. Standing there for an hour looking down on me working. Like I was supposed to be afraid of him. 'Glad to see the Guinness isn't affecting your work Pat.' Oh yeah, gas man. I laughed 'til I puked. (*Switch.*)

April   Mmm, delicious.

Noel   I'm always telling English people they shouldn't despair. The crisis in your culture is temporary. Trust yourselves. There's more to English society than hooligans and the tabloid press. Mmm, very tasty Julian. There are still a lot of fine solid English qualities, if only you had more faith in them.

Julian   Thank you Noel. That's . . . very kind of you to say so. (*Switch.*)

We don't have to put up with this crap. You're a fucking loony do you know that.

Noel   Who me? Oh only joking, Jack.

June   Excuse me.

She brushes past **Noel** *to the kitchen where* **May** *is cowering.*

June   I'm really sorry, May, lovely to meet you and all that, but honestly we thought we were coming here to meet a potential business associate, not be some sort of post-colonial Aunt Sally.

May   Is it me? Did I mess up with the food?

June   No, no, you're a lovely woman really.

Returns to **Julian**.

May   I'll check the chicken. Less than a minute, I'd say.

June   Right Julian?

Julian   Well, June, has the boy done good?

June   Pukkah. We're well impressed.

Noel   I'm going for seconds. What about you, pet?

April   It was so tasty but I don't have a big appetite. I'd love to take a little look around the apartment.

June   Feel free.

Noel   Been in it long?

Julian   Just two years. We love it.

June   If only we could keep it. Not very likely.

April *gets up to look around.*

Julian (*warning*)   June.

Noel   What's that?

Julian   Show April round darling.

June   She's fine.

April   Yes, I'm fine, I'll just have a wander. (*Switch.*)

April *goes into the kitchen.*

Noel   You're going nowhere.

June   You are unbelievable. Do you always treat your guests this way? Barracking, accusations, insults –

May   Oh no. We've never had English people over before.

June   I'd keep it that way if I were you. (*Switch.*)

We're even more delighted you came tonight because frankly we haven't been entertaining very much of late. You see, we are no longer people to be seen with.

Julian   June!

June   Pariahs wouldn't be too strong a word, to be perfectly honest.

Noel   Oh dear – what's happened?

June   Where to start?

Julian   Shouldn't we wait – ?

June   No.

Julian   At least until we are –

June   No Julian.

Julian   Okay. Okay. (*Switch.*)

If that's all we'll be off thank you bye.

Noel   May, will you ever get that food on the table.

May   Coming. Twenty seconds. Less.

Noel   There you go. Twenty seconds. Now come on and we sit down.

Julian   No.

June   We've rather lost our appetite. Can you blame us? (*Switch.*)

I mean it was hardly our fault that various Eastern European banks went to the wall, taking our funds with them. A lot of funds.

Noel   Ah yes.

June   When the Russian mafia moved into Vilnius, they raked our office with machine-gun-fire to encourage us to accept their 'protection.'

Julian   Frightening as fuck I tell you.

June   But the real turning point was when our greediest New Labour client finds out that one of the Sundays is snooping around his financial affairs. He panics, runs to confess his sleazy sins to Emperor Blair, who of course arranges for him to resign quietly, and then puts the revenue dogs on our tail. Anything else?

Julian   May as well put figures on it. They're looking for nearly a million.

Noel   Euro?

Julian   Hm? Oh no, no, no, sterling.

Noel   A million sterling. In tax?

June   Yes. Her Majesty's loyal servants are very insistent.

Julian   The Queen is demanding her tribute. And we ain't got it to give.

Noel   Well, I'm very sorry to hear you're having problems.

Silence. **Julian** *and* **June** *look at each other.*

May *(head through the door)*   Nearly there. Five seconds.

April *(head through the door)*   Love the worktops – real granite yeah?

June   Mhm

April   Love them, love the lighting, love the tiles? *Love* the hob. (*Exits.*)

June   Look, Noel. You're a man of the world. I'm sure you knew we invited you up here because we want something.

Noel   I didn't actually. To be honest, I wasn't thinking of anything like that.

Julian   Really?

Noel   You see the truth is, I've always felt guilty about the way I behaved towards you that night in Dublin. So when you called after all this time, I was shocked that you were even willing to talk to me. But of course I know English people, you don't bear grudges. Anyway it seemed to be a perfect oppurtunity for me to move on to step nine.

Julian   Step nine? What are you talking about? (*Switch.*)

The microwave goes ping! **May** *dives to open it.*

Julian   Babbling like a lunatic. You need to get yourself looked at mate, that's my advice.

Noel   Oh you think so – you think so – mate.

Julian   Yes, bit of a complex going on there. A lot of bad head stuff you need to let go of.

May *appears reluctantly, steaming dish in hand.*

May   Now, Ballymaloo Coq. Loads of it.

As **May** *goes to the table,* **Julian** *and* **June** *go for the front door.*

June   Sorry May. We're going.

Noel   Just you listen to me for a minute. Just you give me a hearing . . . Were you ever on the Greek Islands?

Julian   What?

Noel   The Greek islands?

Julian   (*sighs impatiently*) Oh, Christ.

June   Let him have his fun. Yes, once.

Noel   Have a good time?

June   We had a lovely time.

Noel   Nice and relaxing, easy-going? They're very friendly the Greeks.

June   Yes, very much so.

Noel   Nicest people. How's the grub May?

May   Well it's fine but –

Noel   Grand. They'll be eating in a minute. Last time I was there was the summer of 1986. San Torini.

May   Oh, it was gorgeous.

Noel   The local taverna had set up a TV, especially to watch the World Cup matches. And it was great because there was Irish, Greeks, Swedes and Danes, Germans of course, Scots. Only the one English Couple, a bit boring but grand –

May   They were lovely I remember. Caroline was her name –

Noel   Here's the thing I want to tell you. The night England were playing Argentina, a huge crowd turned up. It was jammed, there must have been people from a dozen countries there, fantastic atmosphere. But I'll tell you, do you know the really interesting thing?

Julian   Let me take a wild guess. They were all cheering for Argentina, yah?

Noel   Yes, but more than –

Julian   And when Maradona got his Hand of God goal, everyone was so delighted. It was even better that he had cheated, more fun, 'cause that really stuck it to the English, just what they deserved. Am I close at all? Is that the big story you have for me? All those people from all those countries with just one thing in common. They hate the English . . .

Noel   That's right.

Julian   Well there you go. Heard that one before. Good night.

Noel   So it doesn't matter to you at all? You couldn't care less what people think about you?

Julian   That's football. You shouldn't confuse it with real life.

Turns to go. Looks back.

Julian/Noel (*together*)   It's much more important than that.

Both are surprised at the other. For one moment male bonding wins out over everything else.

Julian   And let me tell you something, you old Irish bigot. Not so long ago the Beeb had one of those polls to vote for the greatest goal of all time – do you know what won?

Noel   No.

Julian   Maradona's second goal from that game.

Noel   Really? Ye voted for Maradona?

Julian   Yes.

Noel   After what he did. Number one?

Julian   Yes.

Noel   Fair play . . .

Julian   Yes – we're famous for it actually.

May   Of course you are.

Noel   OK.

Julian   Now if you don't mind.

Noel   The truth is, I need a favour.

June   Interesting approach.

Noel   I know. I'm pissed. Sorry. (*Pause.*) Please. Sit down. Eat. I need this favour.

May   I'm really sorry over the delay. He wouldn't have drank half as much if you weren't hanging around for so long, waiting for me to get dinner on the table, would you love. He'll be fine now with the bit of food in him. Go on.

Julian *and* **June** *look at each other.*

As they move to sit, **April** *sticks her head in.* **May** *starts to serve.*

April   Your colour schemes are so vibrant. Hope you don't mind me snooping around. I just love seeing how other people live. It must be the journalist in me.

May   To be honest, he just got a bit over-excited, and that always makes him drink faster. We don't entertain that often and then suddenly to have two people over from England, especially friends of the Minister, well it's a bit of a whirl really. Is it all right?

June   It's lovely.

Julian   Gorgeous.

May   Not too much cream?

Julian   Not at all.

June   Certainly not.

May   It's just that it seemed like an awful lot in the recipe – she's a divil for the cream Darina – double cream too, you know.

June   I think it's quite delicious.

May (*chuffed*)   Well now, I'll have a little taste myself. Eat up, Noel. Mmmm it's not bad is it. It's all right?

Julian   It's perfect, May.

Noel   It'll fill a gap.

He goes to pick up his wine glass. **May** *puts a hand gently on his, to stay him.* **Noel** *looks as though he's about to hit her but he controls himself. (Switch.)*

You see there is no point in simply giving up alcohol. You must examine every aspect of your life, and come to a clear and ruthless understanding of what brought you to this place. You must learn to know yourself all over again.

Julian   Sounds bloody brave.

Noel   It is a road you must travel carefully, step by step. Always asking, 'why?' and 'who?' 'Why did I do the things I did, and who along the way have I offended?' (*Switch.*)

Don't worry May no more trouble.

May   I know. Now, what's it you work at Julian?

Julian   Well – actually June and I run a company together.

May   No! Isn't that great?

Julian   June is an accountant by profession, so she's the financial expert.

May   Lovely.

Julian   And I'm an ex-journalist, so I have useful contacts I suppose, that I picked up along the way.

May   That sounds like a great combination. I'm always on at Noel to let me put in a few hours a week in his place, but sure I'm talking to the wall. Look at them now Noel, business partners.

June   Julian is being very modest. He was more than just a journalist. He was a very highly-placed foreign correspondent. In fact we met in Berlin in '89.

May (*impressed*)   When the wall was coming down? Now isn't that something to look back on? (*Switch.*)

Noel   I must revisit my shame and I must make amends.

Julian Good God, how long does that take?

Noel That depends on how determined I am.

June Well as far as we're concerned, there is nothing to apologise for.

Noel Oh no. On the contrary.

Julian Nothing for you to worry about.

Noel Thank you, but I cannot let myself off the hook as easy as that.

April *looks in again.*

April The bedroom curtains – the linen – exquisite.

May So romantic. To be young in Berlin in 1989.

June Actually it was.

Julian Rather went sour very soon after.

June Not us – the political scene.

Julian A lot of people making a lot of quick money. Nothing I wrote was going to change that.

May Oh sure, I know you can't believe what you read in the papers.

June So we became the naked materialists.

May Sorry?

Julian June says I'm the Jamie Oliver of international finance.

June Do you know Jamie Oliver? Julian has something of that laddish bonhomie, shameless self-promotion, fantastic niche marketing.

Julian And some talent perhaps.

June Of course. I'm the financial brain though. Dull but dogged.

Julian   Actually that is true. I'm merely the front man.

Noel   Enough shite talk. Sorry, but you know, I don't know what you're on about. Anyway. The Minister told me to get in touch. He said you were the ones to look after everything.

June   You owe him some money I presume?

Noel   Do you presume? (*Catches himself.*) Sorry, ah yes. Yes.

May   Who – who do you owe money to?

Noel   May please. Clear up these will you.

May   I know you – you're just trying to get rid of me. Honestly. Come on June, we'll have our own chat in the kitchen.

May *gathers up plates and brings them to the kitchen.* **June** *on the one hand is appalled at the idea of being in the kitchen washing dishes when there is business being done. On the other she really doesn't want to offend* **May**. *She shrugs and stands up.* **Julian** *amused, holds out a plate for her to bring.* **June** *snatches it off him.*

June   Agree nothing without me.

Noel   Ho Ho Ho! (*Switch.*)

Noel   (*sighs heavily.*) You see it has to be treated seriously. It's no use trying to wriggle out of things or pretending that you can't remember certain shameful incidents.

Julian   Right, yeah . . . but really there's no –

Noel   So . . . here I am.

Julian   I see. So . . . how long have you been . . . ah, dry, I suppose.

Noel   I have not had a drink for 1,326 days.

Julian   Impressive. (*Switch.*)

Noel *lifts glass and downs his wine in one go. Pours again.*

Julian   Very impressive. A bit frightening.

Noel   No, I'm fine now. I'll behave myself.

May   Your Julian is lovely.

June   Thanks.

Julian   So you owe our friend some money.

Noel   Yes.

Julian   How much?

Noel   A hundred thousand pounds.

Julian   Mmm, he did you big favours. Still, simple enough to handle.

May   You seem like a real romantic couple.

June   Well . . .

Julian   You see we provide a service mainly used by a certain kind of politician. The pragmatic kind, I suppose you'd say.

May   Noel and I used to be very romantic. 'Course that was then.

Julian   Nowadays politicians aren't so keen on having bundles of dirty fivers slipped to them in a pub. They prefer something more sophisticated. So we accept the money on their behalf, filter it through our system, and then provide our clients with a decent legal and acceptable payment on a regular basis. They can even declare it as an interest. Pay tax on it if they really want. Call it consultancy.

Julian *writes something on a piece of paper.*

May   Now it's just work and money.

June   And the odd drink?

May   I know. Do you think he has a problem?

June   I'd . . . keep an eye on it.

Julian   Okay. Here's what'll happen. I give you the names and numbers of five bank accounts in different banks in different Eastern European cities. Like so . . .

May   I mean we haven't had a holiday together in years, I'd love us to take off somewhere exciting. We can well afford it.

Julian   You will deposit £20,000 in each bank on different days over the space of a fortnight or so.

May   Like, we met in Majorca. You met in Berlin. That's much classier.

Julian   Technically, you are paying consultancy fees for property advice in these very turbulent but potentially lucrative markets.

May   All those places in Eastern Europe.

Julian   Such as Bucharest –

May   Budapest –

Julian   Sofia –

May   Prague –

Julian   Tbilisi –

May   Moscow –

Julian   Etc . . .

May   You know what I mean?

June   The reality is a bit seedier though . . .

Julian   The money is funneled back to the relevent politician . . .

June   . . . Ugly . . .

Julian   . . . less interest and commission of course.

June   . . . sad

May   I suppose . . . still . . .

Noel   Sounds very well organised.

Julian   Everyone's happy so far.

Noel   But it's a bit more complicated in my case.

Noel *fills his glass and drinks.*

June   Do you mind if I go back in. I want to hear what –

May   Of course, go on. I'll finish these in no time.

June *returning.*

Julian   Luckily I don't need to know any details. In fact I prefer not to.

Noel   It's all to do with this shopping-centre development. Of course there's the usual crowd of protestors –

Julian   I don't want to know. We'll keep this simple.

Noel   Will you just listen to me?

Julian   Try and understand, you don't need to –

Noel   For Christ's sake! Do you English ever listen? – I mean . . .

June   Julian, let him talk.

Noel   Thank you. To make sure next week's vote on the planning permission goes my way, I made a few contributions to local councillors, mostly small stuff, a couple of thousand here and there. Your friend and mine got the biggest lump of that, 30,000 nicker in cash. Anyway fine, that's the way it goes. Money well spent as far as I'm concerned . . . At the last minute – the vote is next Tuesday by the way – he comes looking for another £100,000. I tell him fuck off of course. But he means it. He's not just chancing his arm. I tell him I don't have it, which is the truth. I've borrowed every which way to set this up. I haven't a bean to give him. 'Nothing to do with me pal', he says . . . I know what's happened. Someone else has come in. Barney Doyle or some bollocks is trying to gazump me.

Offering him more money. 'I'll owe it to you,' I said, 'sure you know once I get the planning permission I'll be good for it'. 'Don't I know it,' says he, 'no way Jose, once you get the planning permission you're off and running, you're no good to me then'. 'I don't fuckin' have it,' I said, 'are you listening to me at all, you can check it out. There's nowhere I can raise a £100,000 at this stage' . . . 'Maybe I can help you out there,' he says to me . . .

Julian   I see. And suggested you talk to us.

June   So what's the proposal exactly?

Noel   You . . . let him know the money is there for him.

June   Do you mean, we give you a loan?

Noel   Well sort of, but sure I'll never even see it. He'll get the planning permission put through. Once I have that, I can raise more funds, and I pay you back as soon as I'm good for it, with interest.

Julian   Are you serious?

Noel   Of course. Step nine is a really crucial part of the programme, because you see, if I can't face up to the bad things I did in the past, if I can't bring myself to go to the person or persons that I offended and say, 'here is what I did wrong, and I am sorry.' If I can't do that, how can I believe I have any serious intention of changing my life? And when I remember how I treated you all those years ago, the anger inside me – (*Switch.*)

You're going to say no aren't you? You are, aren't you!

– the appalling language I used towards both of you – (*Switch.*)

You fuckpigbastard –

The unwarranted prejudice I expressed – (*Switch.*)

Fuckin English. I should have known, why did I lower myself to ask a fucking Englishman for anything. You wouldn't give the steam off your piss to an Irishman, would you?

May *runs in.*

May   Ah not again. Noel get in here, please.

Noel   And then the final indignity I caused you to suffer. Don't worry, I'm not avoiding the worst part –

Julian   You don't have to mention that.

Noel   I can hardly bring myself to say it out loud –

May   Noel, shut up now.

Noel   But I have to. It's part of step nine.

May   Get in here immediately.

Noel   I have to admit to everything and take full responsibility.

Julian   (*very agitated*) It's fine. Just let it go!

June   Sorry Noel. Give us a moment okay. Can you excuse us?

May   Noel!

Noel   Of course take your time. (*Switch.*)

I'm coming all right. (*Switch.*)

Noel *follows* **May** *into their kitchen, while* **Julian** *and* **June** *go into theirs.*

As soon as **Noel** *walks into the kitchen,* **May** *shoves a mug of black coffee into his hand. He drinks, sullen, morose, silent.*

June   This is fantastic?

Julian   What?

May   I'm at the end of my tether. I really am –

June   (*taking out bombe*)   You heard him. He wants to make amends. We have him right there.

May   What's the point of inviting people over for a
pleasant night's chat –

Julian   I'm not so sure.

May   And then just turn into a mad person?

Julian   I'm getting panicky again.

June   Why? He's a completely different person.

May   Always showing people your bad side.

Julian   But not in a good way. He's – he's weird – and
her, that April – what's that about?

June   Who cares. He realises how badly he behaved the
last time.

May   Is it you can't help yourself?

Julian   I suppose.

June   He wants to make amends.

May   I don't know.

Julian   Does he really?

June   Jules relax, we're pushing an open door.

May   If you'd only let people see that lovely, funny,
generous side of you.

June   Now's the time. Focus.

May   Go back in there and behave yourself . . .

June   It's you he feels guilty about. I'll get the coffee and
pudding ready –

May   And by the time I come in with the dessert –

June   You sweet-talk him.

May   You create a lovely relaxed ambience.

June   (*checks watch*)   I'll give you about five minutes.

May   Now can you please do that?

Julian/ Noel   Okay, I'll try.

Noel *and* **Julian** *return to the dining room simultaneously.*

Noel   So . . .

Julian   So . . .

Noel   May is just organising the bit of apple tart.

Julian   Sure, sure . . .

Noel   I'm looking forward to that now – a lovely home made dessert and coffee and a nice relaxing chat. Where is ahm . . . ?

Noel *looks around*

Julian   June?

Noel   Yes, of course, sorry. June.

Julian   The loo . . . (*Switch.*)

April must be . . . ?

Noel   Still looking around. Women and houses, ha – well flats.

Julian   Right, yeah. Ha, ha, ha . . .

Noel   Ha . . . ha . . . ha . . .

Julian   Hey, it's . . . it's great having you over, after so long.

Noel   I'm glad I came. Time changes everything you know.

Julian   Indeed, yes.

Noel   Now, I still have to talk to you about the worst part of all.

Julian   No really –

Noel   My nadir.

Julian   Actually I'd prefer to talk to you about something else.

April *returns*.

April   It's so fabulous.

Julian   Thank you. Although we can't take much credit for anything.

Noel   You really like it honey?

April   I love it. It's roomy, it's tasteful.

Noel   Good. Sorry Julian, you were saying.

Julian   Oh. Well, it's a business sort of a thing . . .

Noel   Don't worry. April and I have no secrets. We couldn't build our relationship any other way. Say whatever you like.

Julian   Okay. It's about – well it's . . . it's a situation that's developed. Noel, we have some cash hidden away but technically we're bankrupt. In the long run, if those wankers in revenue have anything to do with it, it's probably prison. So we have to get out really. And we thought, I mean it was June thought of it, but I'm all in favour – we thought – Ireland. We like Ireland. It's a good place to, ah, well, to get away from it all. And if we could find a way to set up there, transfer whatever assets we have left, maybe, you know, we'd get by.

Noel   And you'd like my help in some way (*Switch*.)

It's a big favour I know. I'm straight up about that. All I can say is, I'd do it for you.

Julian   Really?

Noel   Yes, yes, if it came to it. Jesus yes, never let it be said if a friend was in trouble –

Julian   But we're not friends, we've only just met. I'm one of those English bastards, aren't I –

Noel   Ah don't be like that. Anyway I'll pay up. I'm as good as my word. It's just time I need.

Julian   See we don't do bridging finance as such. It's not really our thing. (*Switch.*)

If we set up what seemed to be an Irish-owned business, her Majesty's tax inspectors couldn't get at it.

Noel   But it can't be an Irish business unless – ah.

Julian   Unless the registered owner is an Irish citizen. All the better if it's a highly regarded Irish businessman. Of course June and I will be the beneficial owners. We are asking you for a very big favour, I know. (*Switch.*)

An enormous favour actually. I mean it makes no sense, what's in it for June and I? Risk, hassle.

Noel   Listen to me. I don't have a hundred thousand to give this fucker now, do you get it? That's the way it is. So if I don't pay him, I don't get the planning permission. Nothing comes your way, you don't get your cut. We all lose out. But the other way –

Julian   It's one little backhander among many. We'll survive.

Noel (*losing it again*)   Why are you being such a – sorry, sorry. (*Breathing heavy.*) You want me to beg, is that it?

Julian   Oh please.

Please. It would save our skins.

April   I'm sorry, Julian. I have to speak up here.

Julian   What?

April   I think what you're asking Noel to do is illegal?

Noel   I'm afraid so.

Julian   Of course it's illegal. That's why it's such a big favour.

April   Noel.

Noel   I know honey. (*Turns to* **Julian**.) Then it's out of the question. I can't do anything illegal.

April   It's the kind of thing that could destroy his recovery.

Julian   Ah, now, now, now, now – wait now. Hold on now. Okay, right, yes, yes I see your point – I understand your reasons. Your recovery, okay. Very important clearly.

Noel   More than that.

Julian   But surely, surely . . . listen to this now, surely that . . . issue only applies if there is personal gain involved. But in fact you would be doing this for a good motive – to help someone else out.

Noel (*kindly smile*)   No. It doesn't work that way (*Switch.*)

What then? What do I have to do? How embarrassing does it have to be? What'll make you happy?

Julian   It's nothing personal, why are you making it personal? We don't give loans.

Noel   'We don't give loans.' Well, give one this time you . . .

Julian   Calm down. Think about this in a business-like way –

Noel   The planning permission comes through, I'm on the pig's back, I'll pay you back double if you like. Is that business-like enough?

Julian   I don't doubt it. Please understand where I'm coming from.

Noel   Please understand where I'm coming from. I'd love to help you out. You know how guilty I feel about the way I treated you. In fact – April?

April   Yeah.

Noel   I think you like it, do you?

April   What? Oh. Yes. It's gorgeous.

Noel   Okay. Julian, I think we can help in one way.

Julian   Go on.

Noel   I came here to make amends for past wrongs. Partly. But we also came so that April and I could have a look at this apartment. You see, I own this building.

Julian (*deep shock*)   What!

Noel   Never been inside it until tonight. Acquired it a couple of years ago as an investment property. Very good investment too. Very good yield.

Julian *is stunned.*

Julian   Ooooh! (*Switch.*)

> I wish you well with all your investments but as I say –
>
> **Noel**   Give us a break here. You won't regret it.
>
> **Julian**   Please. This is too embarrassing. (*Switch.*)

Utterly humiliating. June!

Noel   Don't feel that way.

Julian   We invited you to dinner, and you came to view the property?

Noel   April and I had been talking about a place in London for a while, and so when June called and I saw the address, I thought, this is a sign.

Julian   Just go please. Get out of our apartment. June! (*Switch.*)

> Time for us to be off. Darling!
>
> **Noel** (*breathing heavily*)   Hagh – ah – hagh – ah. No hold on. May is organising coffee and cake.
>
> **Julian**   Sorry Noel. We've said everything and it's very late. June!

Noel (*still in discomfort*)   Baked it herself. She'll ah she'll be very disappointed.

Julian   It's been a long night. Where are our coats?

Noel   You're not leaving here until I say so. (*Switch.*)

We like this apartment. The location is perfect.

April   And now that I've had a good look around, I love the space, love the layout, love the fittings.

Julian   June!

June   Coming.

Noel   So if you move out immediately, rather than wait for your lease to run out, we'll compensate you financially. Say . . . 300,000 Euro. No strings. And you could tell us how to pay you so it would be . . . most beneficial to you right now. That'd be all right, wouldn't it April?

April   That'd be fine. That's not crossing the line.

Julian   Jesus Christ this is a nightmare. (*Switch.*)

You really won't take no for an answer will you?

Noel (*heartburn*)   It'll cost you nothing, nothing. A few weeks credit, and it's my life, my whole fucking life, that's what we're talking about here, you smug English bollocks. Oh, aah! . . .

Noel *clutches his stomach, as* **May** *comes from her kitchen.*

May   Ah now Noel –

Noel   Eugh!

Noel *lurches forward and throws up all over* **Julian** *who turns away in disgust.*

Julian   You fucking Irish lout –

Julian *thumps* **Noel** *who keels over,*

as **June** *comes from hers bearing the Castro bombe ice cream dessert, and coffee pot.*

May   Ah Noel no!

June   Ta raaa! Pudding!

Julian *turns into the Castro bombe and coffee which smashes all over his chest.*

June   Oh!

Noel *has collapsed behind a sofa.* **May** *goes to him.*

May   Oh, this is the end it really is.

June   Darling I'm so sorry.

Julian *stands there, his whole front covered with a combination* of vomit *and ice-cream dessert.* **May** *and* **June** *go to wipe him.*

Julian   Stop. Let me alone!

May /**June**   Sorry.

Julian *picks up a napkin and makes very obviously unsuccessful efforts to clean himself. Silence.*

Julian   Believe it or not, June. This is not the worst of it.

(Switch.) Turns to **May**.

You. Tell your blaggard husband that he can find someone else to pay his backhanders for him.

(Switch.) **Julian** *turns to* **Noel**.

You (*he is lost for words*) . . . he owns our apartment.

June   What are you talking about?

Julian   He wants to chuck us out.

Noel   For 300,000 euro. *(Switch.)*

Julian   £100,000 he wants from us so he can slip it to politicians in return for favours.

May (*utterly shocked*) This is terrible. This is desperate. (*Switch.*)

June This is appalling. You're a scumbag.

April I sense a bit of an atmosphere. I think we should go Noel.

Noel You're right, honey. (*To* **June**.) It'll give you a bit of time to consider our suggestion.

They go to collect their coats.

June We don't need to make our minds up, do we Julian? (*Switch.*)

Jules, let's give him the money.

Julian What? I'd let him die first.

June Give him his little loan.

Julian Have you lost your mind?

June You've assaulted him, Jules. Look, don't you see? If we do this, it makes us better than they are. We take the moral high ground. He'll hate that. (*Switch.*)

Fucking Irish fucking lowlife. (*Switch.*)

Julian I like the sound of that. (*To* **May**) When your husband sobers up, tell him this . . . (*Switch.*)

We know what you used to get up to. We have evidence. We could expose you.

April We all have pasts we're ashamed of in some way.

Noel The thing is to be sorry, make amends. (*Switch.*)

Julian He can pay us back our money into these five bank accounts. (*He offers her the scrap of paper.*) Twenty thousand in each. We don't ever have to deal with each other again.

May A hundred thousand pounds? You should be ashamed of yourself.

Julian   Sorry? What about your husband? (*Switch.*)

(*To* **Noel**.) Aren't you ashamed at all?

Noel   Our tribunals are over Julian. They've reported.

April   Noel was vindicated.

Noel   Well, in fairness, honey, I think I got a bit of a slap on the wrist.

May   I'm disgusted. I'm disgusted at these things going on in my house.

Noel   It's a very generous offer.

May   I'm not touching that. (*Switch.*)

Noel   You should think about it. (*Switch.*)

May   Dirt money. (*Switch.*)

Noel   300,000 euro. The offer stands.

Julian   You were in the gutter. We did you a favour. Think where you'd be if we hadn't done that for you.

June   Julian, let it go.

Julian   You were a dead man.

Noel   Possibly . . . (*Switch.*)

May   Noel, Noel, get up, will you please!

April   But . . . this is now.

And they exit.

Julian   What do we do? . . . June?

June   Treat them with the contempt they deserve. Make them feel small and vulgar and unimportant. And . . . eventually, accept their offer.

May   I'd have expected more from you, a lovely English couple like you. I thought you were respectable.

Julian *and* **June** *put on their coats.*

June   Goodnight, May. I'm . . . sorry.

And they exit. **May** *surveys the scene. Looks down at* **Noel**. *She pulls him up on to the sofa.*

May   Oh, Noel. I'm so ashamed of you. So ashamed. All the effort I made and for what? What a mess.

Blackout.

Curtain.